Microsoft Visio 2013 Essentials

Michelle N. Halsey

ISBN-10: 1-64004-152-4

ISBN-13: 978-1-64004-152-3

Contents

Chapter 1 – Opening and Closing Visio

In this chapter, you will learn to open Visio. You will also explore the Visio interface, including the new Backstage view. Finally, you will learn to create a blank drawing and close Visio.

Opening Visio

Use the following procedure to start Visio.

Step 1: Press the Windows key on the keyboard to open the Desktop menu.

Step 2: Select the Visio icon.

Step 3: Next, highlight the Microsoft Office program group. Select **MICROSOFT VISIO 2013**.

Understanding the Interface

Visio 2013 has a new interface that builds on interface from the previous version of Visio. Visio 2013 uses the **RIBBON** interface that was introduced in Microsoft Office 2007 applications. Each **TAB** in the **RIBBON** contains many tools for working with your drawing. To display a different set of commands, click the tab name. **BUTTONS** are organized into groups according to their function.

In addition to the TABS, Visio 2013 also makes use of the Quick Access Toolbar from the MS Office 2007 applications.

The File tab is a new feature that opens the Backstage View. The new Backstage View will be discussed in the next topic.

Below is the Visio interface, including the Ribbon, the Slides tab, the Slides pane, the Quick Access toolbar, and the Status bar.

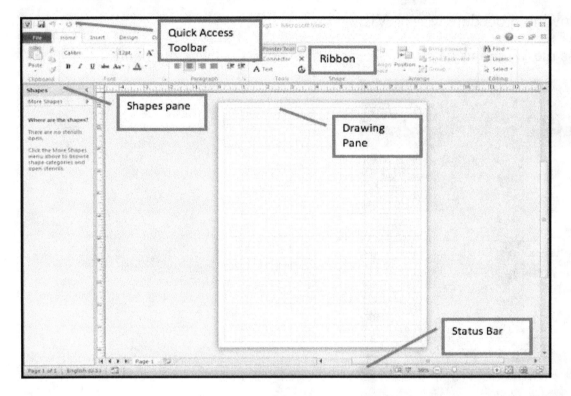

- The Shapes panel shows a thumbnail of shapes and/or stencils.

- The Drawing pane is where you can view and edit the entire drawing.

- The Status Bar provides information about your drawing and has additional tools for making changes to the view.

The Quick Access Toolbar appears at the top of the Visio window and provides you with one-click shortcuts to commonly used functions. By default, the Quick Access Toolbar contains buttons for Save, Undo and Redo.

Use the following procedure to customize the contents of the Quick Access toolbar.

Step 1: Click the arrow icon immediately to the right of the Quick Access toolbar.

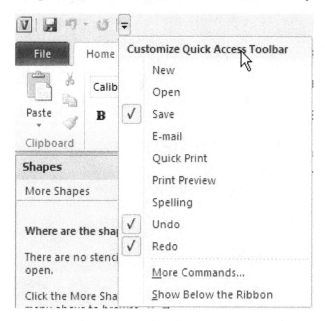

Step 2: Add an item to the Quick Access Toolbar by selecting it from the list. You can remove an item by reopening the list and selecting the item again.

If you select More Commands, Visio opens the Visio Options window.

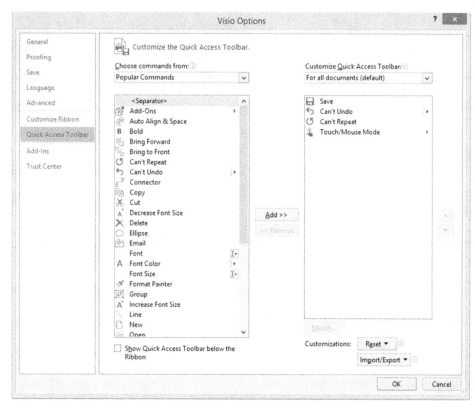

To add a command, select the item from the list on the left and select **ADD**. Select **OK** when you have finished.

Using Backstage View

Select the **FILE** tab in the Ribbon to open the Backstage view. The Backstage view is where you will find the commands for creating, saving, opening, and closing files, as well as information about the file. The Backstage view includes new interfaces for printing and sharing your drawings. The Options command is also available to open a new screen for setting your Visio Options.

Use the following procedure to open the Backstage View.

Step 1: Select the **FILE** tab on the Ribbon.

Visio displays the Backstage View, open to the Info tab by default. A sample is illustrated below.

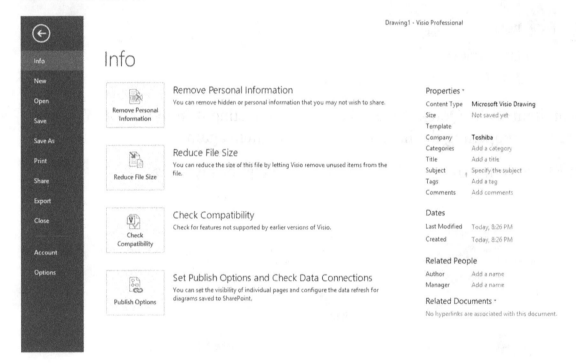

Creating a Blank Drawing

The New tab of the Backstage view provides several options for creating new drawings. The Blank Document option is at the bottom of the screen under "Other Ways to Get Started."

Use the following procedure to create a blank drawing.

Step 1: Select the **FILE** tab on the Ribbon.

Step 2: Select the **NEW** tab in the Backstage View.

Step 3: Select **BLANK DRAWING**.

Step 4: Select CREATE.

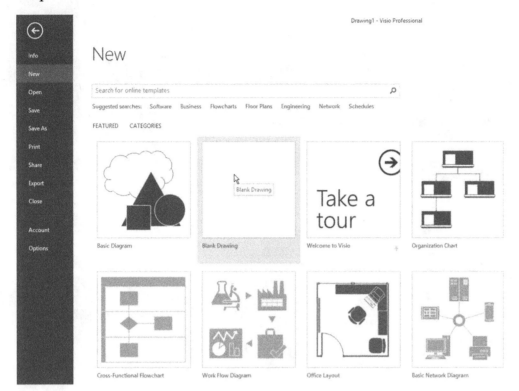

Closing Visio

Use the following procedure to close Visio from the Backstage View.

Step 1: Select the FILE tab on the Ribbon.

Step 2: Select the EXIT command in the Backstage View.

Chapter 2 – Working with Files

This chapter will cover some of the specific tasks you can do using the new Backstage view. First, it is important to save your work regularly to protect your work. The Backstage view allows you to open an existing file from anywhere on your computer or network. You can also easily open drawings you have recently opened. This chapter will also cover creating a drawing from a template. Finally, this chapter discusses how to close a drawing when you have finished working on it.

Saving Files

The Backstage view includes the Save and the Save As commands.

Visio will remind you to save your drawing if you attempt to close it without saving it first.

Use the following procedure to save a drawing.

Step 1: Select the **FILE** tab on the Ribbon.

Step 2: Select the **SAVE** command in the Backstage View.

If the drawing has not yet been saved, the Save As dialog box opens, so that you can name the drawing and select a location to save it. The Save As dialog box is illustrated below.

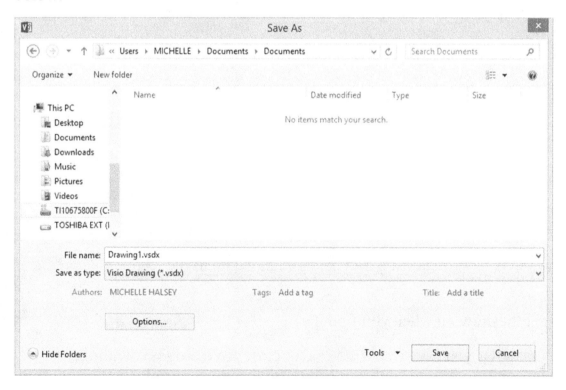

Step 3: Enter a name for the document in the **FILE NAME** field.

Step 4: Use the **SAVE IN** drop down list to help you navigate to the location where you want to save the file.

Step 5: Select **SAVE**. Or you can select **CANCEL** to close the dialog box without saving the drawing.

The Backstage view returns to the background after the save operation is complete.

Opening Files

Use the following procedure to open a drawing.

Step 1: Select the **FILE** tab on the Ribbon.

Step 2: Select the **OPEN** command in the Backstage View.

The Open dialog box opens, so that you can navigate to the location of the desired drawing and select it. The Open dialog box is illustrated below.

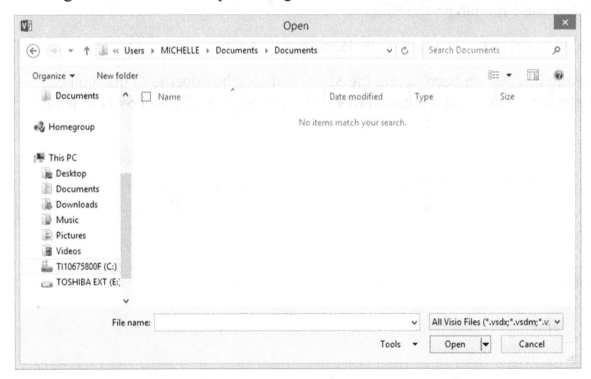

Step 3: Use the **LOOK IN** drop down list to help you navigate to the location where the file is located.

Step 4: Highlight the drawing when you find it.

Step 5: Select **OPEN**. Or you can select **CANCEL** to close the dialog box without opening the drawing.

The Backstage view returns to the background after the open operation is complete.

Closing Files

Use the following procedure to close a drawing.

Step 1: Select the **FILE** tab on the Ribbon.

Step 2: Select the **CLOSE** command in the Backstage View to close the current drawing.

The Backstage view returns to the background after the close operation is complete.

Switching Between Files

The Switch Windows tool on the View tab of the Ribbon provides a quick way to switch between drawings. You can also switch using the icon on the Status bar.

Use the following procedure to switch from one drawing to another.

Step 1: Select the **VIEW** tab from the Ribbon.

Step 2: Select **SWITCH WINDOWS**.

Step 3: Select the file you want to view.

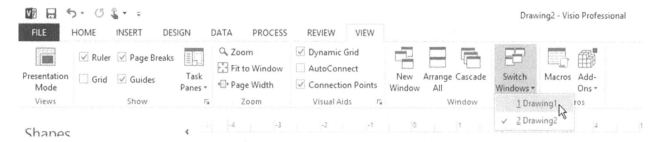

Switch Windows tool on the Status bar.

Chapter 3 – Setting Up Your Screen

In this chapter, you will learn how to set up your Visio screen. You have different elements to help you create your drawing, which you can show or hide as needed. This chapter will explain how to add, move, and delete a guide. It will also explain how to change the ruler settings and the grid settings.

Showing and Hiding Screen Elements

Visio's ruler, grid, guides, and connection points can be toggled on or off with the View menu. The Task panes can also be shown or hidden depending on the current need.

Use the following procedure to hide the grid lines.

Step 1: Select the **VIEW** tab from the Ribbon.

Step 2: Clear the **GRID** box.

The Task Panes

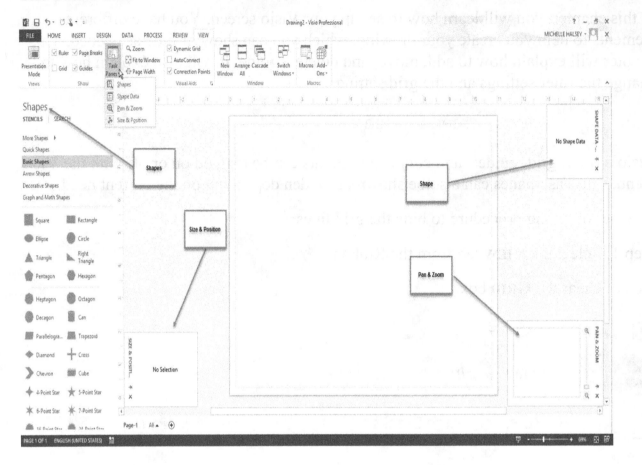

Adding a Guide

Guides help you line up the shapes in your drawing. They do not appear on the final drawing when you print or save the drawing as a picture. You can add as many guides as you need, either horizontally or vertically, to help you with your drawing.

Use the following procedure to add a guide.

Step 1: Click and drag the ruler to create a guide.

Step 2: Drag it to the desired location. The guide appears as a dotted line. Release the mouse button to place the guide. The guide is still selected in the second illustration.

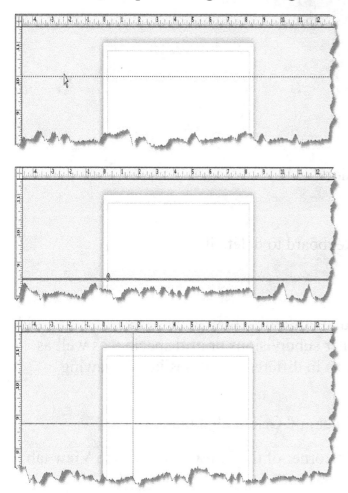

Moving or Deleting a Guide

Use the following procedure to move a guide.

Step 1: Click the guide you want to move. The small circle containing a plus sign, plus the larger blue highlighting of the guide indicates that it is selected.

Step 2: Drag it to the desired location. The guide appears as a dotted line. Release the mouse button to place the guide in the new position.

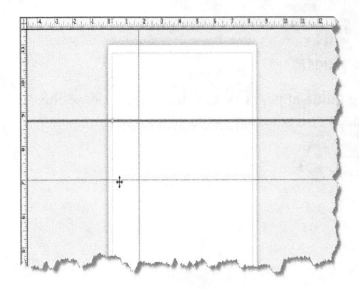

Use the following procedure to delete a guide.

Step 1: Click the guide you want to move.

Step 2: Press Delete or Backspace on the keyboard to delete it.

Changing Ruler and Grid Settings

The Rulers and Grid dialog box allows you to customize how you use the ruler and grid in the Visio canvas. You can control the ruler subdivisions or grid spacing, as well as set the origins to help with measuring objects in different positions in the drawing workspace.

Use the following procedure to open the Ruler and Grid dialog box.

Step 1: Select the square at the bottom right corner of the **Show** group on the **View** tab of the Ribbon.

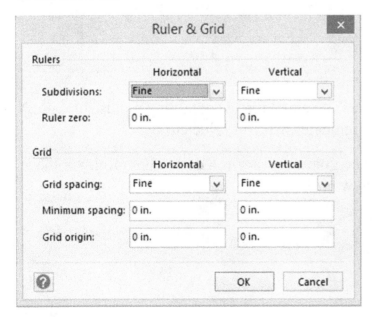

Chapter 4 – Your First Drawing

In this chapter, you will create your first drawing. Drawings consist of shapes. This chapter will cover how to find the right shape and place it on your drawing. You'll learn how to add text to shapes. You'll learn how to work with shapes, including resizing, moving, and deleting shapes. This chapter will also cover using the Tools group, which helps with refining your shapes.

Finding the Required Shape

The Shapes pane allows you to search through different categories to find the shape that you need. You can expand or collapse categories as you use them. You can use the Search Shapes tool to search for shapes within Visio, and you can even look for more shapes online.

Use the following procedure to open a stencil.

Step 1: Select **More Shapes** from the Shapes pane.

Step 2: Select a Category.

Step 3: Select the Shape stencil you want.

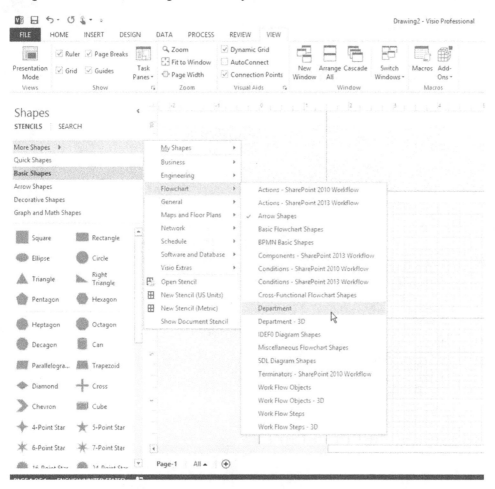

Visio displays the shapes in that stencil in the Shapes pane.

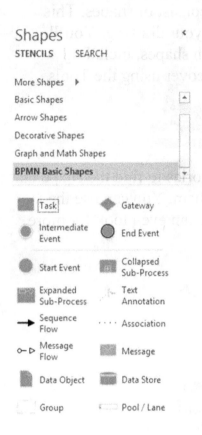

Use the following procedure to search for shapes.

Step 1: Select **More Shapes** from the Shapes pane.

Step 2: Select **Search for Shapes.**

Visio displays a Search field.

Step 3: Enter text to describe the shape you want to find.

Step 4: Press the Enter key or select the magnifying glass to begin the search.

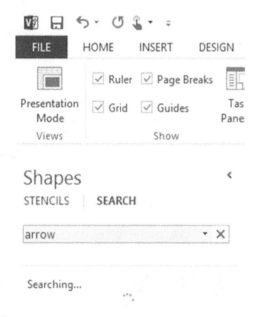

If there are many matches, Visio displays the following warning.

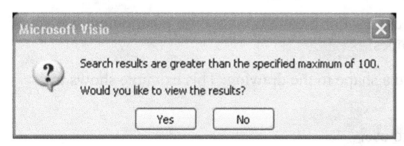

Step 5: Select **Yes** to continue.

Visio displays the matches in the Shapes pane. Use the scroll bar to scroll down to see all of the matching shapes.

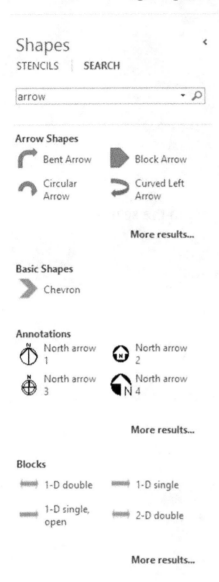

Placing the Shape in the Drawing

It is easy to drag shapes to your drawing. For greater control over positioning, use your guides or grid to help place the shapes.

Use the following procedure to add a shape to the drawing. This example shows the Glue to Guide feature.

Step 1: Click the shape you want to use.

Step 2: Drag it to the drawing canvas.

Step 3: If you want to glue the shape to a guide, position it so that the red box (es) are visible.

Step 4: Release the mouse button to position the shape.

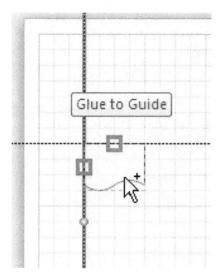

Adding Text to a Shape

Text can bring additional meaning to your diagram. To add text to a shape, simply double-click the shape.

Use the following procedure to enter text in a shape.

Step 1: Double-click the shape.

Step 2: Type your text.

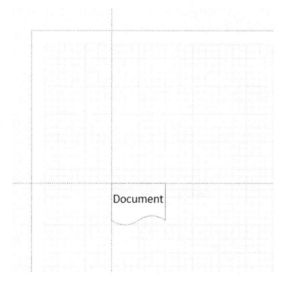

Shapes can be adjusted by size and position on the drawing. You can also simply delete a shape that is not working for the drawing.

Use the following procedure to resize a shape.

Step 1: Click the shape to activate it. Visio displays handles around the shape to show that it is active.

Step 2: When you move your cursor to one of the corner handles, the cursor changes to a double-arrow. Click and drag the handle to resize the shape proportionally. Release the mouse when the shape is the size you want.

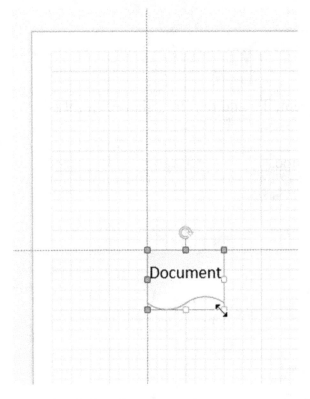

Use the following procedure to move a shape.

Step 1: Click the shape to activate it. Visio displays handles around the shape to show that it is active.

Step 2: Drag the shape. The cursor appears as a cross of double arrows.

Step 3: Release the mouse when the shape is in the new position.

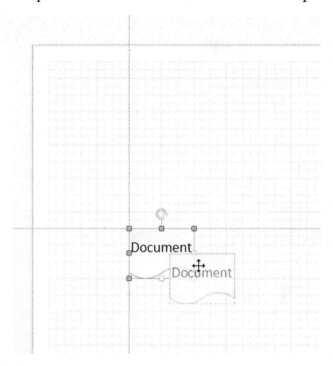

Use the following procedure to delete a shape.

Step 1: Click the shape to activate it. Visio displays handles around the shape to show that it is active.

Step 2: Press the Delete key.

Using the Tools Group

The Tools group includes a number of tools to help you complete your drawing.

- The Pointer tool is used to select shapes and other objects.

- The Connector tool allows you to connect shapes.

- The Text tool allows you to select text in a shape or type free-form text on your drawing.

- The Rectangle, Ellipse, and Line tools allow you to draw basic shapes.

- The Connection Point tool allows you to add, move, or delete connection points on shapes.

The Text Block tool allows you to move, resize, or rotate the text block on a shape.

Tools group on the Home tab of the Ribbon.

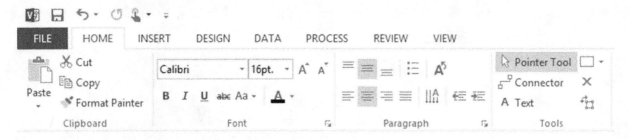

Use the following procedure to connect two shapes.

Step 1: Select the Connector tool from the Home tab of the Ribbon.

Step 2: Click the shape you want to connect. The cursor changes to a red square to show that you are using a connection point.

Step 3: Drag the connector to the shape you want to connect. Release the mouse to connect the shapes.

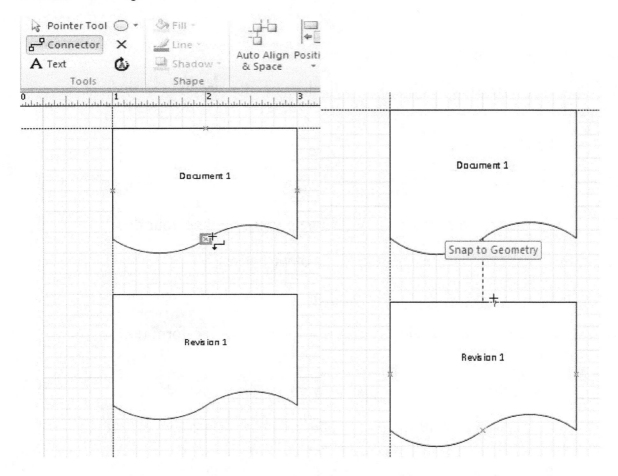

Chapter 5 – Basic Editing Tasks

The Visio 2013 editing tools make editing your drawing a breeze. This chapter covers how to cut, copy and paste text or shapes, as well as duplicating a shape. It also explains how to find and replace text, such as when you want to change a word or phrase throughout your drawing. Finally, this chapter explains how to check your text for spelling errors.

Using Cut, Copy, and Paste

Visio 2013 makes it easy to adjust drawings, including a new drawing based on a template, or a drawing started by you or another Visio user.

Before you cut or copy, select the text you want to edit by highlighting it. If you want to cut or copy a shape, just click it to select it.

The cut command deletes the selected text or shape from the current location, but allows you to move it somewhere else.

The copy command allows you to copy the selected text or shape, leaving it in the current location, but also allowing you to include it somewhere else.

The paste command allows you to include the text or shape you have cut or copied at the cursor's current location.

Click anywhere on a slide to paste text or shapes.

Use the following procedure to cut and paste text.

Step 1: Double-click the shape with the text you want to cut.

Step 2: Right click the mouse to display the context menu and select cut.

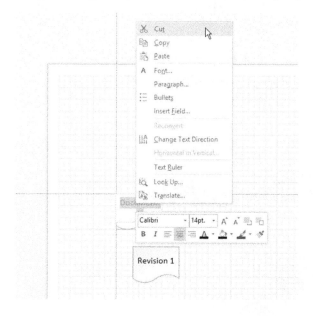

Step 3: Double-click the shape where you want to paste the text. You can also paste the text on the drawing without placing it in a shape. Just click the drawing.

Step 4: Right click the mouse to display the context menu and select **Paste**.

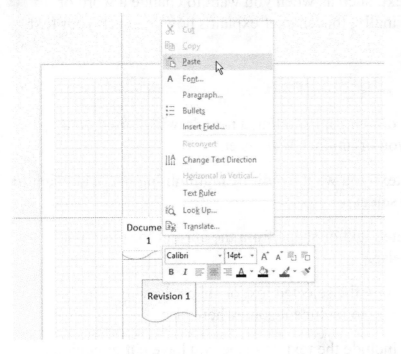

Use the following procedure to copy and paste text using the keyboard shortcuts.

Step 1: Double-click the shape with the text you want to cut and press the Control key and the C key at the same time.

Step 2: Double-click the new shape or click the drawing to paste the text outside a shape.

Step 3: Press the Control key and the V key at the same time.

Use the following procedure to copy and paste a shape.

Step 1: Click the shape you want to copy to select it. Notice the cursor changes to a cross with arrows in all directions and the shape handles are visible.

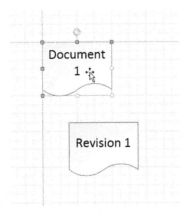

Step 2: Select **Copy** from the Ribbon, the context menu, or by using the keyboard shortcut.

Step 3: Click the drawing.

Step 4: Select **Paste** from the Ribbon, the context menu, or by using the keyboard shortcut.

Step 5: Move the shape to the new location.

Duplicating Shapes

Instead of dragging a shape from the Shapes pane or copying and pasting, you may want to duplicate all of the features of a shape you have adjusted. Duplicating a shape makes an exact copy of the selected shape(s).

Use the following procedure to duplicate a shape.

Step 1: Click the shape to activate it. Visio displays handles around the shape to show that it is active.

Step 2: Select the **Paste** tool from the Ribbon. Select **Duplicate**.

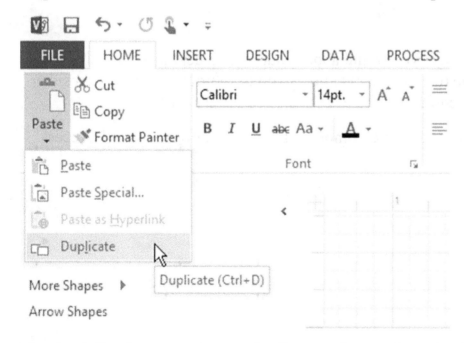

Use the following procedure to duplicate a shape using a keyboard shortcut.

Step 1: Click the shape to activate it. Visio displays handles around the shape to show that it is active.

Step 2: Press the CTRL key.

Step 3: Drag the shape. The cursor appears as an arrow with a plus sign to show that you are making a copy.

Step 4: Release the mouse when the new shape is in position.

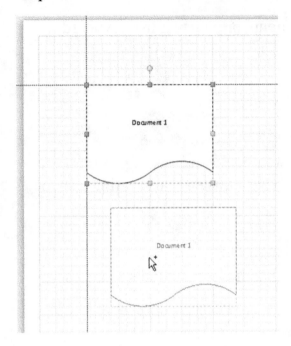

Using Undo and Redo

If you make a mistake or change your mind about your most recent task in Visio, you can undo the command. The redo command allows you to return the command results back to your drawing. The redo command also allows you to repeat tasks.

The Undo and Redo commands are so common that they appear on the Quick Access toolbar by default.

Use the following procedure to undo your most recent command.

Step 1: Select the Undo command from the Quick Access Toolbar. If there is more than one item listed, you can select more than one item to undo all selected actions.

Use the following procedure to redo the last command or repeat it.

Step 1: Select the Redo command from the Quick Access Toolbar.

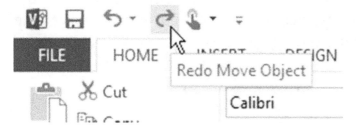

Finding and Replacing Text

The Find dialog box allows you to quickly find text in your drawing. You can also search for other types of information, such as the name of a shape you used.

The Replace dialog box provides several options for finding multiple instances of text in your drawing, and replacing them, if necessary.

Use the following procedure to find text.

Step 1: Select **FIND** from the Editing group on the Home tab of the Ribbon to open the Find dialog box. Select **Find**.

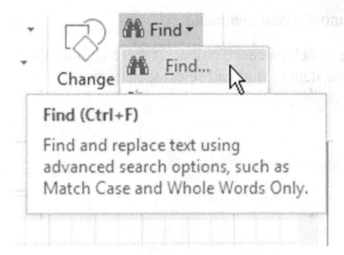

Find (Ctrl+F)

Find and replace text using advanced search options, such as Match Case and Whole Words Only.

Step 2: Enter the exact text you want to find in the **FIND WHAT** field.

Step 3: Indicate where Visio should search for the text: the current selection, the current page, or all pages.

Step 4: Indicate whether the text is **Shape text**, **Shape data**, **Shape Name** or a **User-defined cell** by checking or clearing the boxes. **Shape text** is checked by default, because that is the most common selection.

Step 5: If desired, check the **Match Case** box to find only instances with the same capitalization.

Step 6: If desired, check the **Find Whole Words only** box to find the whole word. Leaving this box unchecked will find any instance of that group of letters. For example if you search for the word box, but have the **Find Whole Words Only** box unchecked, Visio will find instances of box, as well as instances of "boxes" and "boxed." Check the **Match character width** box to only find instances of the text with the same character spacing.

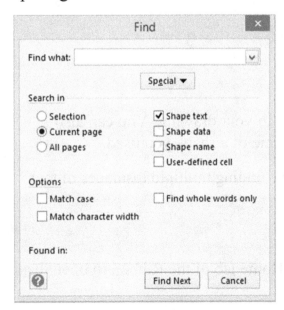

Step 7: Select **Find Next**.

Visio highlights any matching items for you to review. Select Find Next again to find the next instance.

Visio displays the following message when it has finished searching.

Step 8: Select **OK**.

Step 9: Select **Cancel** to close the Find dialog box.

Use the following procedure to replace text.

Step 1: Select **FIND** from the Editing group on the Home tab of the Ribbon to open the Replace dialog box. Select **Replace**.

Step 2: Enter the exact text you want to find in the **FIND WHAT** field.

Step 3: Enter the replacement text in the **REPLACE WITH** field.

Step 4: Indicate where Visio should search for the text: the current selection, the current page, or all pages.

Step 5: If desired, check the **Match case**, **Match character width**, and/or **Find Whole Words only** boxes.

Step 6: Select **FIND NEXT** to find the next instance of the item.

Step 7: When Visio highlights the item, select **REPLACE** to delete the "find" item and paste the "replace" item.

Step 8: Select **CLOSE** when you have finished. Or select **CANCEL** to close the dialog box without making any replacements.

Use the following procedure to replace all instances of an item.

Step 1: Select **FIND** from the Editing group on the Home tab of the Ribbon to open the Replace dialog box. Select **Replace**.

Step 2: Enter the exact text you want to find in the **FIND WHAT** field.

Step 3: Enter the replacement text in the **REPLACE WITH** field.

Step 4: Indicate where Visio should search for the text: the current selection, the current page, or all pages.

Step 5: If desired, check the **Match case**, **Match character width**, and/or **Find Whole Words only** boxes.

Step 6: Select **REPLACE ALL**.

Step 7: Select **CLOSE** when you have finished. Or select **CANCEL** to close the dialog box without making any replacements.

Visio replaces all instances of the item.

Checking Your Spelling

Use the following procedure to open the Spelling dialog box.

Step 1: Select the **SPELLING** tool from the **PROOFING** group in the **REVIEW** tab of the Ribbon.

Discuss the buttons on the Spelling and Grammar dialog box.

- The Ignore button allows you to keep the word as the current spelling, but only for the current location.

- The Ignore All button allows you to ignore the misspelling for the whole drawing.

- The Add allows you to add the word to your dictionary for all Visio drawings.

- The Suggestions area lists possible changes for the misspelling. There may be many choices, just one, or no choices, based on Visio's ability to match the error to other possibilities.

- The Change To field shows the currently highlighted suggestion .Or you can use it to enter the correct spelling.

- The Change button allows you to change the misspelled word to the highlighted choice in the Suggestions area. You can highlight any word in the Suggestions area and select Change.

- The Change All button allows you to notify Visio to make this spelling correction any time it encounters this spelling error in this drawing.

- The Options button allows you to set the options to have Visio automatically correct certain types of errors.

Chapter 6 – Formatting Shapes

In this chapter, you'll learn how to customize your shapes. This chapter explains how to change the shape outline and fill. We'll also cover how to add shadows, how to change the line types and ends, and even how to modify the corners.

Changing the Outline

You can choose any color for your lines. The Shape group includes a gallery to choose one of the following for your line color:

- **Automatic** – Makes the line black.

- **Theme Colors** – Includes a palette of colors based on the drawing's theme.

- **Standard Colors** – Includes a palette of 10 standard colors.

- **More Colors** – Opens the Colors dialog box to choose from more colors or to enter the values for a precise color.

You can also choose from a number of standard line widths for your lines or shape outlines.

Use the following procedure to select a color for their lines from the gallery.

Step 1: Select the shape you want to change.

Step 2: Select the arrow next to the Line tool on the Ribbon to display the gallery. Or select the same tool from the context menu (appears when you right click a shape).

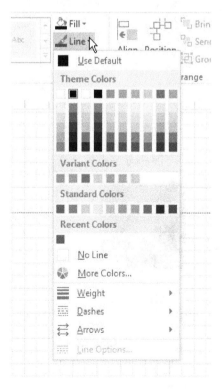

Step 3: Select the color to change the line color.

Use the following procedure to open the Colors dialog box.

Step 1: Select the shape you want to change.

Step 2: Select the arrow next to the Line tool on the Ribbon to display the gallery. Or select the same tool from the context menu (appears when you right click a shape).

Step 3: Select **MORE COLORS** to open the Colors dialog box.

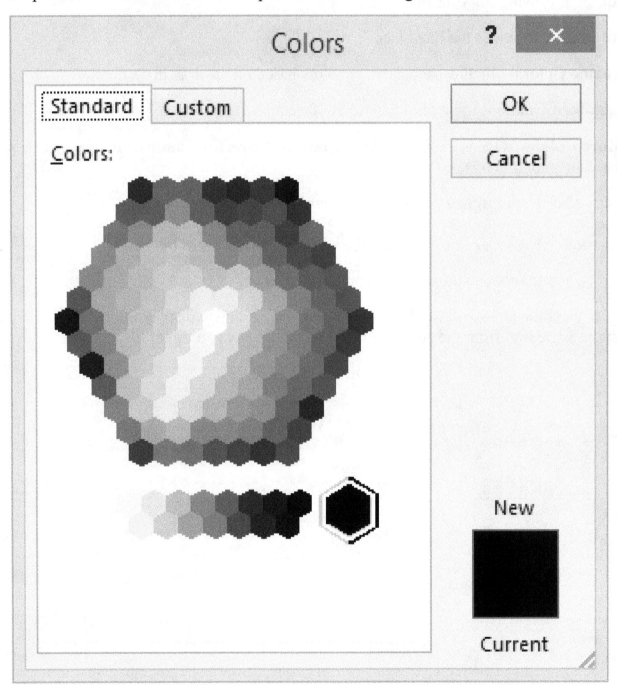

In the Standard Colors dialog box, simply click the color and select **OK** to use that color.

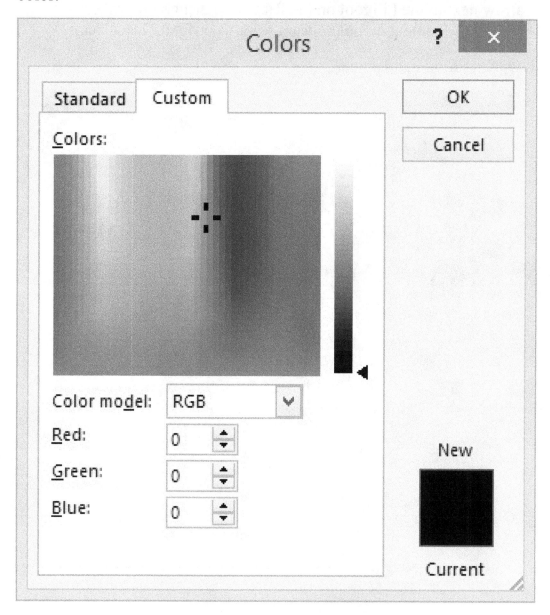

In the Custom Colors dialog box, you can click the color, or you can enter the red, green, and blue values to get a precise color. When you have the color you want, select **OK**.

Changing the Fill

You can choose the same or a different color for the fill in your shape. The Fill dialog box allows you to select the details for your shape fill, including various transparency levels for patterns. The dialog allows you to preview your changes before applying them.

Use the following procedure to open the Fill dialog box.

Step 1: Select the shape you want to change.

Step 2: Select the arrow next to the Fill tool on the Ribbon to display the gallery. Or select the same tool from the context menu (appears when you right click a shape).

Step 3: Select Fill Options from the Ribbon.

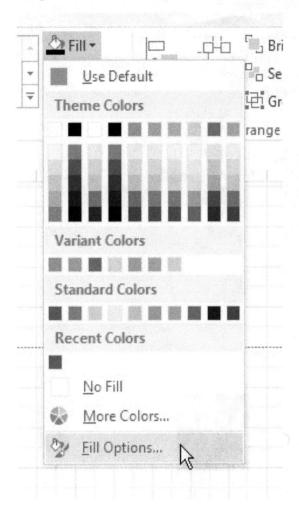

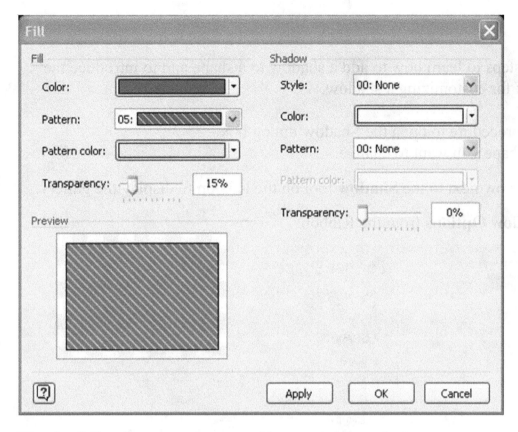

Use the following procedure to add a pattern to a shape.

Step 1: Select the shape you want to change.

Step 2: Select the arrow next to the Fill tool on the Ribbon to display the gallery. Or select the same tool from the context menu (appears when you right click a shape).

Step 3: Select Fill Options from the Ribbon.

Step 4: Select the color for the background from the **Color** drop down list.

Step 5: Select the style of pattern from the **Pattern** drop down list.

Step 6: Select the color of the pattern from the Pattern Color drop down list.

Step 7: Select the Transparency for the fill color and pattern. Use the slider to select a value from 0% to 100%.

Step 8: Select **Apply** to apply the fill to your shape.

Step 9: Select **OK** to close the Fill dialog box.

Adding Shadows

Use the following steps to learn how to add a shadow to a shape and to introduce the Shadow dialog box for customizing a shadow.

Use the following procedure to open the Shadow dialog box.
Step 1: Select the shape you want to change.

Step 2: Select the arrow next to the **Shadow** tool on the Ribbon to display the gallery.

Step 3: Select **Shadow Options** from the Ribbon.

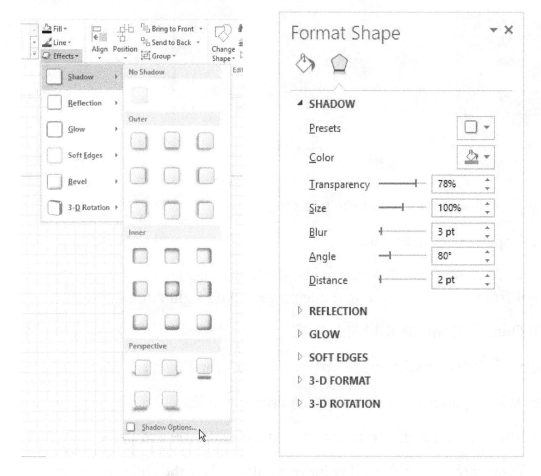

Changing Line Types and Ends

You can use a variety of line types (such as dashes) and end types (such as arrows) on your lines.

Use the following procedure to change line types.

Step 1: Select the shape you want to change.

Step 2: Select the arrow next to the Line tool on the Ribbon. Or select the same tool from the context menu (appears when you right click a shape).

42

Step 3: Select **Dashes**.

Step 4: Select the type of line you want to use.

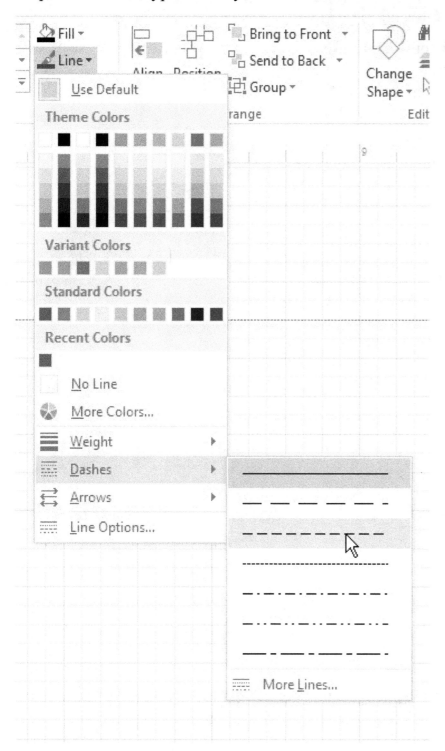

Use the following procedure to change the line end.

Step 1: Select the shape you want to change.

Step 2: Select the arrow next to the Line tool on the Ribbon. Or select the same tool from the context menu (appears when you right click a shape).

Step 3: Select **Arrows**.

Step 4: Select the type of end you want to use.

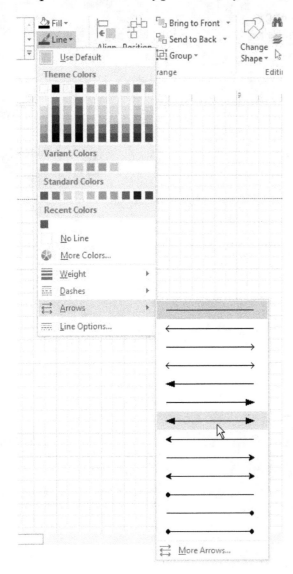

Modifying Corners

The Line dialog box allows you to change a number of details for your shape lines, including modifying the corners. You can select from a gallery of different corners or customize the rounding by measurement.

Use the following procedure to apply round corners.

Step 1: Select the shape you want to change.

Step 2: Select the arrow next to the Line tool on the Ribbon. Or select the same tool from the context menu (appears when you right click a shape).

Step 3: Select **Weight**, **Dashes** or **Arrows**.

Step 4: Select **More Lines** or **More Arrows**.

Step 5: Select the type of corner that you would like to use in the **Round corners** area.

Step 6: Select **Apply** to apply the changes to your shape.

Step 7: Select **OK** to close the Line dialog box.

Chapter 7 – Formatting Text

Visio 2013 allows you to enhance your text in many ways. In this chapter, we'll discuss the different types of formatting, as well as cover the most basic types of formatting for your text. This includes the font face, size, and color, as well as adding effects to the text. We'll also discuss how to use the Format Text dialog box.

Changing Font Face and Size

You can easily change the font face to any font installed on your computer. You can use the Font group on the Ribbon, or you can use the context menu that appears when you select text and right-click the mouse.

The Font face list includes the theme fonts first, and then the most recently used fonts, then the other fonts installed on your system in alphabetical order.

The font size is measured in points, which is unit of measure in typography.

Use the following procedure to change the font face and size using the Ribbon tools.

Step 1: Select the text you want to change. Or you can select the shape.

Step 2: Select the arrow next to the current font name to display the list of available fonts.

Step 3: Use the scroll bar or the down arrow to scroll down the list of fonts.

Step 4: Select the desired font to change the font of text.

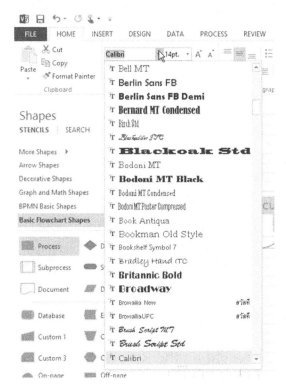

Step 1: With the text still selected, select the arrow next to the current font size to see a list of common font sizes.

Step 2: Use the scroll bar or the down arrow key to scroll to the size you want and select it. You can also highlight the current font size and type in a new number to indicate the font size you want.

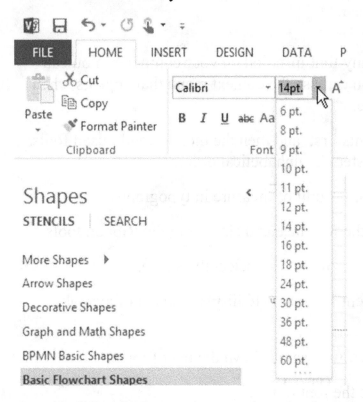

Use the following procedure to view the font context list that appears when you select text.

Step 1: Select the text you want to change.

Step 2: Right-click to display the context menu appears.

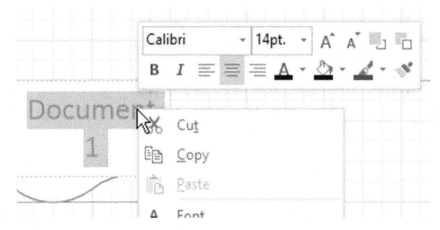

Step 3: Select the new font face or font size just as you would on the Ribbon.

Changing the Font Color

You can choose any color for your text. The font group includes a gallery to choose one of the following for your font color:

- **Theme Colors** – Includes a palette of colors based on the document's theme.

- **Standard Colors** – Includes a palette of 10 standard colors.

- **More Colors** – Opens the Colors dialog box to choose from more colors or to enter the values for a precise color.

Use the following procedure to select a color for their fonts from the gallery.

Step 1: Select the text you want to change.

Step 2: Select the arrow next to the Font Color tool on the Ribbon to display the gallery. Or select the same tool from the context menu (appears when you right click).

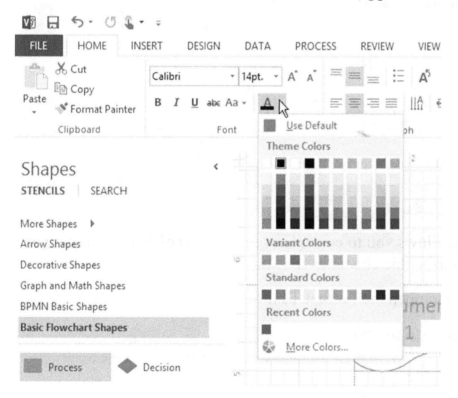

Step 3: Select the color to change the font color.

Adding Effects

You can choose several effects for your text. The font group on the Ribbon and the font context menu allow you to easily change the font to:

- Bold

- Italic

- Underline

- Strikethrough

Use the following procedure to add text effects.

Step 1: Select the text you want to change.

Step 2: Select the effects tool you want to use from the Ribbon. Bold and Italic are also available from the context menu.

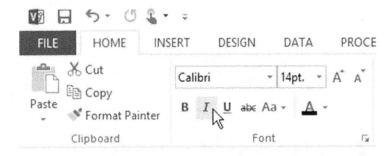

Using the Format Text Dialog

The Format Text dialog box allows you to control several aspects of font formatting at one time. It also allows you to set the character spacing.

Use the following procedure to open the Format Text dialog box.

Step 1: Select the text you want to format.

Step 2: Select the square at the bottom right corner of the Font group in the Ribbon.

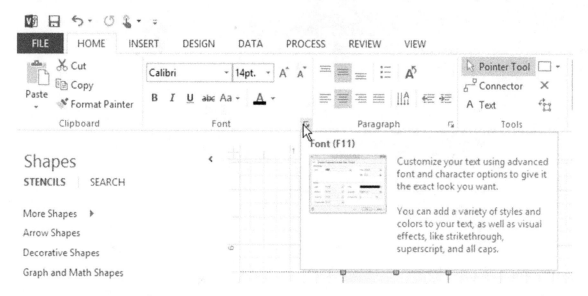

Format Text dialog box Font tab.

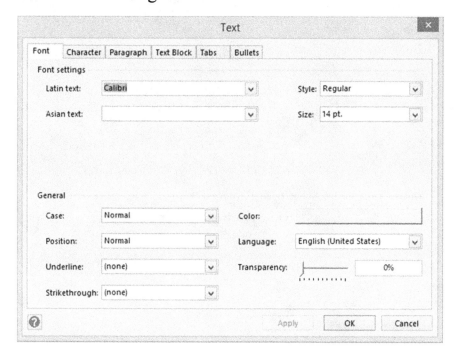

Format Text dialog box Character Spacing tab.

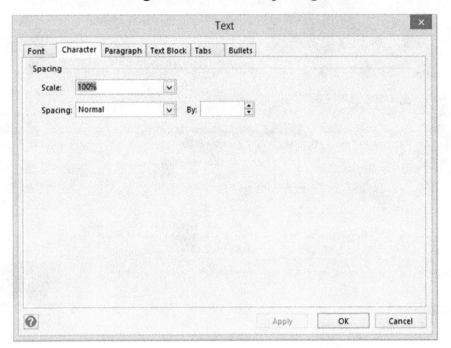

Chapter 8 – Formatting Blocks of Text

In Visio, text resides in blocks, whether it is part of a shape or not. In this chapter, you'll learn how to work with those text blocks. This chapter explains how to set the alignment and change the indents and paragraph spacing. This chapter also explains how to add bullets and numbering.

Setting the Alignment

You can align your text to the left, to the right, or in the center. You can also justify the text. You can also align your text to the top, to the middle, or to the bottom of the text block.

Use the following procedure to adjust the alignment for the paragraph.

Step 1: Click the text block or shape you want to adjust (the text does not have to be selected).

Step 2: Select the desired alignment tool from the Ribbon. You can also select multiple shapes.

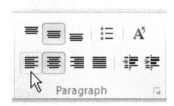

Changing the Indent

You can easily indent your text, or remove an indentation, using the tools on the Ribbon.

Use the following procedure to adjust the indent for text.

Step 1: Click the text block or shape you want to adjust (the text does not have to be selected).

Step 2: Select the desired indent tool from the Ribbon. You can also select multiple shapes.

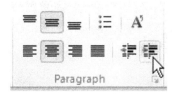

The Paragraph tab of the Format Text dialog box allows you to add space before or after a paragraph. It also allows you to adjust the line spacing within a paragraph.

Use the following procedure to open the Paragraph tab of the Format Text dialog box and adjust the space above, space below, and line spacing options.

Step 1: Click the text block or shape you want to adjust (the text does not have to be selected).

Step 2: Select the square at the bottom right corner of the Paragraph group in the Ribbon.

Step 3: Select the **Paragraph** tab.

Step 4: You can use the up and down arrows to adjust the **Spacing Before** and **after** the paragraph. The arrows adjust the points in typographical increments. You can also enter any number in the **BEFORE** and **AFTER** fields to adjust the spacing more precisely.

Step 6: The **Line** field allows you to select set the line spacing as a percentage. Single spacing would be 100%.

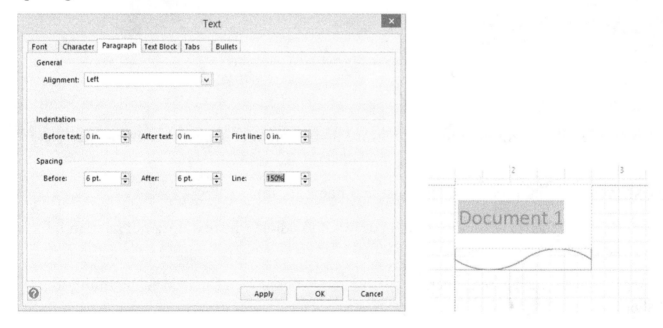

Step 7: Select **Apply** to apply the Paragraph settings to your text block.

Step 8: Select **OK** to close the Text dialog box.

Adding Bullets

The Ribbon includes a tool on the Paragraph group to quickly create a bulleted list. You can also use the Format Text dialog box to use custom bullets.

Use the following procedure to create a simple bulleted list.

Step 1: Select the text block or text you want to turn into a bulleted list.

Step 2: Select the Bullets tool from the Ribbon.

Bullet Library

Step 1: Select the square at the bottom right corner of the Paragraph group in the Ribbon to open the Format Text dialog box.

Step 2: Select the **Bullets** tab.

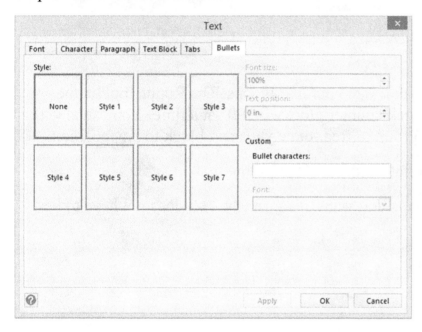

Use the following procedure to create a custom bullet.

Step 1: Select the square at the bottom right corner of the Paragraph group in the Ribbon to open the Format Text dialog box.

Step 2: Select the **Bullets** tab.

Step 3: Select the Font size for your bullet from the drop down list.

Step 4: Enter a text position measurement or use the up and down arrows to select it.

Step 5: Enter the custom bullet character in the Bullet Characters field.

Step 6: Select the font for the bullet character from the drop down list.

Step 7: Select **Apply**.

Step 8: Select **OK** to close the dialog box.

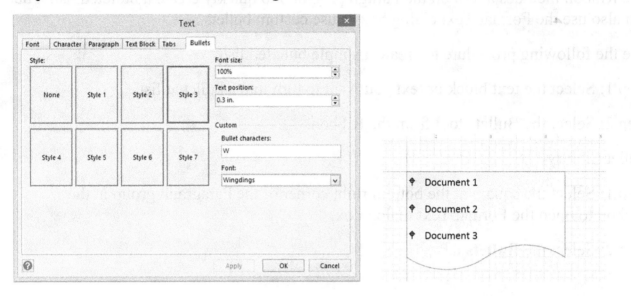

Rotating Text

In addition to aligning text, you can rotate your text blocks. The Rotate tool on the Ribbon rotates your entire text block counter-clockwise 90° at a time. You can also use the Text Block tool in the Tools group to free rotate your text block to any position.

Use the following procedure to rotate text using the Rotate tool.

Step 1. Click the text block or shape you want to adjust (the text does not have to be selected).

Step 2: Select the **Rotate Text** tool.

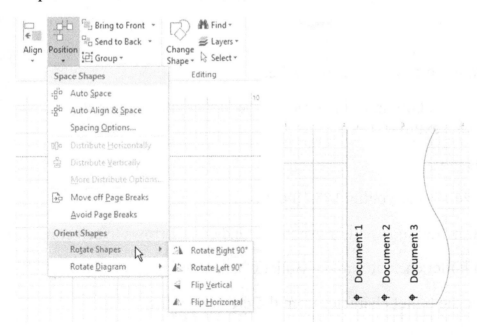

Use the following procedure to rotate text using the Text Block tool.

Step 1: Click the text block or shape you want to adjust (the text does not have to be selected).

Step 2: Select the **Rotate Text** tool.

Step 3: Click the top handle and drag until the text block is rotated as desired. Release the mouse to position the text block.

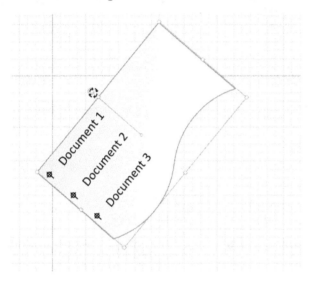

Chapter 9 – Formatting Your Drawing

This chapter explains how to format your drawing. You'll learn how to select multiple objects. This chapter covers how to use the format painter, styles, and themes to further enhance your drawing. You'll also learn how to center your drawing and change your layout.

Selecting Multiple Objects

You can resize, move, or format multiple shapes at once to save time and create a more consistent look to your drawing.

Use the following procedure to select multiple objects.

Step 1: Make sure you are using the Pointer tool.

Step 2: Draw a square around the shapes you want to select. You can also hold down the SHIFT key or CTRL key while clicking multiple shapes.

Visio highlights the selected shapes with a border around the group. Note that in the following example, the top right shape is NOT selected.

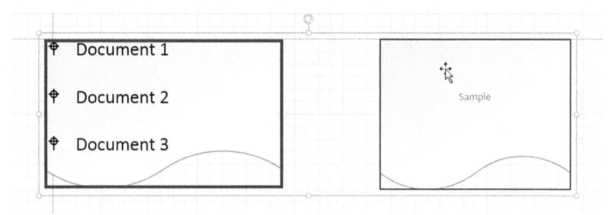

Using the Format Painter

The Format Painter allows you to quickly apply the same formatting from one shape or text block.

Use the following procedure to use the Format Painter.

Step 1: Select the shape or text that has been formatted with the formatting properties that you want to copy.

Step 2: Select the Format Painter tool.

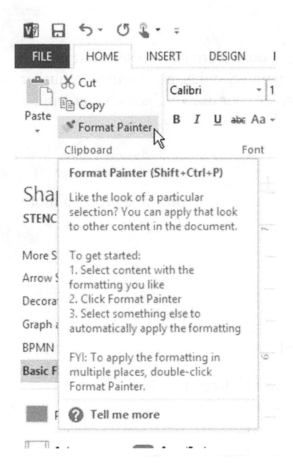

The cursor changes to a Format Painter cursor, as illustrated below.

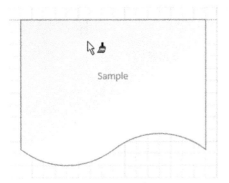

Step 3: Select the shape or text you want to format with the same properties.

The cursor returns to normal after applying the formatting properties once. You can always repeat the process to format more text or other shapes with the same properties.

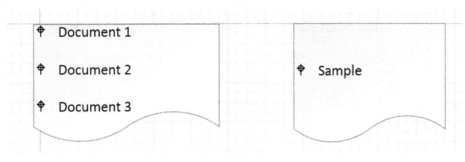

Applying a Theme

Themes control the look and feel of your entire drawing, including the colors, fonts, and shape styles. The drawing previews the themes as you hover over each option in the Themes gallery.

Use the following procedure to change the theme.

Step 1: Select the **DESIGN** tab on the Ribbon.

Step 2: Select the **THEMES** tool from the Ribbon to see the options.

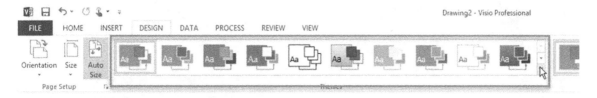

Step 3: Select a Theme from the list.

Using Backgrounds

Backgrounds are another way to customize the look of your drawing. Visio 2013 includes a number of background styles to quickly change the look of your drawing. You select the background style and the color separately.

Use the following procedure to change the background.

Step 1: Select the **DESIGN** tab on the Ribbon.

Step 2: Select **Backgrounds**.

Step 3: Select the background you want to use.

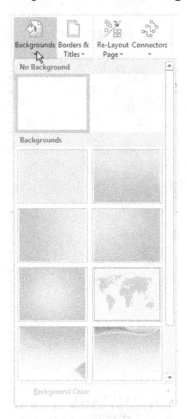

Step 4: Select **Backgrounds** again. Select **Background Color**.

Step 5: Select the desired color from the color gallery.

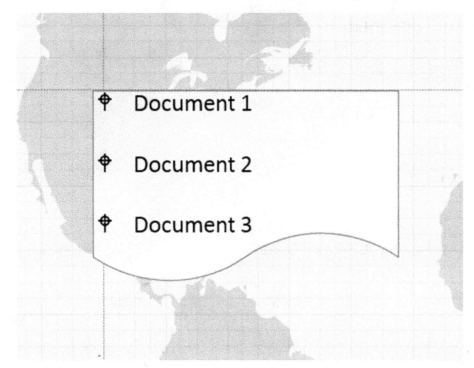

Using Borders and Titles

The Borders and Titles gallery provides another option for giving your drawing a professional polish. The Borders and Title option places a text block to use as a title for the drawing.

Use the following procedure to add a border and title.

Step 1: Select the **DESIGN** tab on the Ribbon.

Step 2: Select **Borders & Titles**.

Step 3: Select the Border and Title layout you want to use.

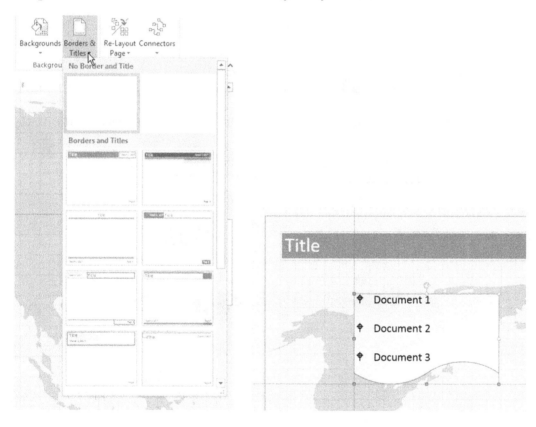

Use the following procedure to change the default text for the border and title.

Step 1: At the bottom of the drawing, there are tabs for the different pages. Click the VBackground-1 page created when you added the border and title.

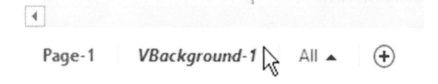

Visio displays the background layer of the drawing.

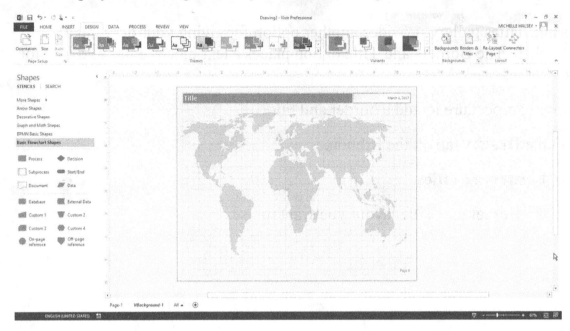

Step 2: Now you can click each Border and Title element and replace or format the text, just as with any other shape.

Step 3: Select the Page 1 tab at the bottom to return to your drawing.

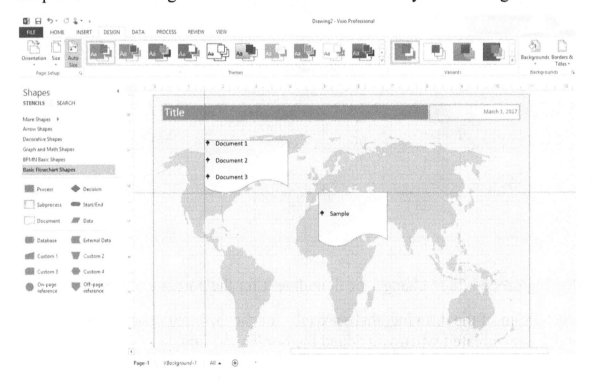

The Re-Layout Page gallery allows you to select from a number of options to reposition the shapes on your drawing. The Configure Layout dialog box provides more precise control over the style, the direction, the alignment, and the spacing concerning your shape placement. You can also control the style and appearance of connectors on this dialog box.

Use the following procedure to view the Re-Layout page gallery.

Step 1: Select the **DESIGN** tab on the Ribbon.

Step 2: Select **Re-Layout Page**.

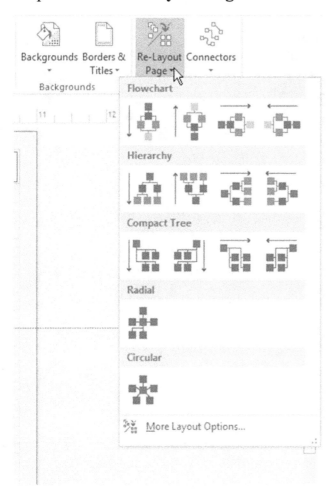

Use the following procedure to view the Configure Layout dialog box.

Step 1: Select the **DESIGN** tab on the Ribbon.

Step 2: Select **Re-Layout Page**.

Step 3: Select **More Layout Options**.

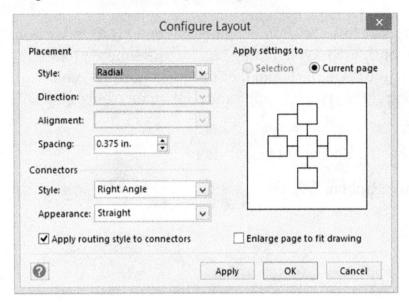

Chapter 10 – Adding the Finishing Touches

Your drawing is almost ready. In this chapter, you'll learn how to validate your drawing and add a legend. You'll also learn how to prepare the drawing for sharing. This chapter explains how to use the Page Setup group. It also explains how to save the drawing as a picture, print the drawing, and email a drawing.

Validating Your Drawing

Validation help ensure that your drawing meets general diagramming or company-specific best practices and/or requirements. You select a set a rules to use for the validation process. Once you have instructed Visio to check the diagram, it displays the Issues window to explain any deviations from the selected set of rules. You can use the Issues window to quickly find the problem shapes. You can even ignore an issue if it does not apply.

Use the following procedure to view the Check Drawing options.

Step 1: Select the **Process** tab.

Step 2: Indicate the rule set by selecting the arrow next to **Check Diagram**. Select **Rules to Check**. Select the rule for that diagram. Or you can select the arrow next to **Check Diagram** and select **Import Rules from**. Then select the rules from another open Visio file.

Step 3: Check the diagram by selecting **Check Diagram**.

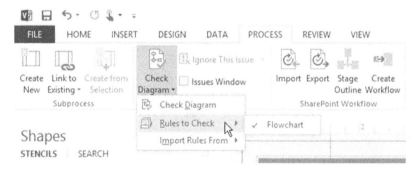

Use the following procedure to view the Issues Window.

Step 1: Make sure that the **Issues Window** box on the Process tab is checked.

Step 2: After you check a drawing, view the Issues window.

Step 3: You can double-click an issue to select that shape on the drawing.

Step 4: To ignore an issue, highlight the issue in the Issues window and select **Ignore This Issue** from the Ribbon.

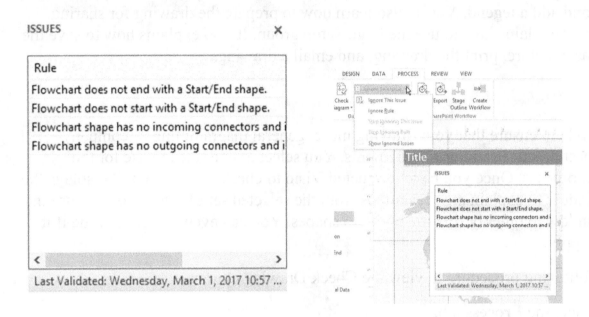

Using the Page Setup Group

The Page Setup Group includes options for determining your page orientation and size. You can have Visio auto size your drawing, based on the layout of the shapes it contains. The Page Setup dialog box allows you to customize your page setup.

Use the following procedure to change the page orientation.

Step 1: Select the **Design** tab from the Ribbon.

Step 2: Select **Orientation**.

Step 3: Select either **Portrait** or **Landscape**.

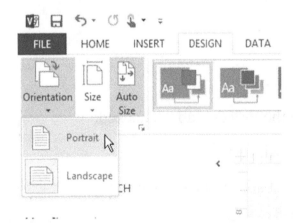

Use the following procedure to change the drawing size.

Step 1: Select the **Design** tab from the Ribbon.

Step 2: Select **Size**.

Step 3: Select a page size from the list.

Page Setup dialog box.

Step 1: Select the **Design** tab from the Ribbon.

Step 2: Select the small square in the bottom right corner of the Page Setup group on the Ribbon to open the Page Setup dialog box.

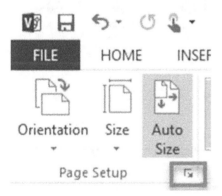

The Print Setup tab allows you to choose the printer paper, zoom level, and whether the gridlines should print.

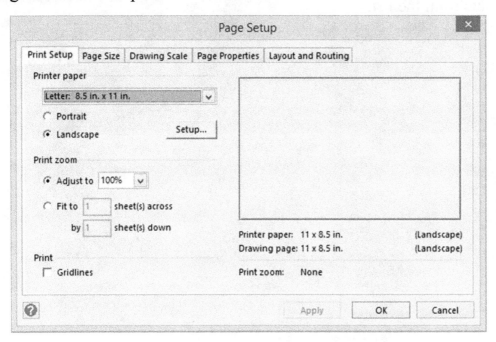

The Page Size tab allows you to choose the page size and orientation.

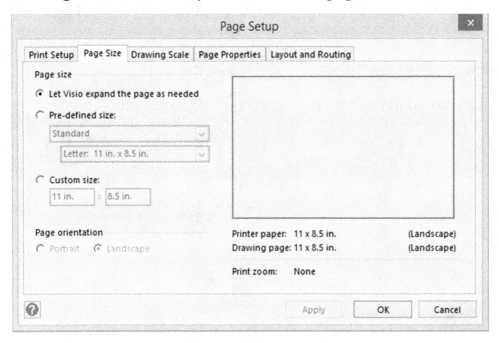

The Drawing Scale tab allows you to set the scale of the drawing.

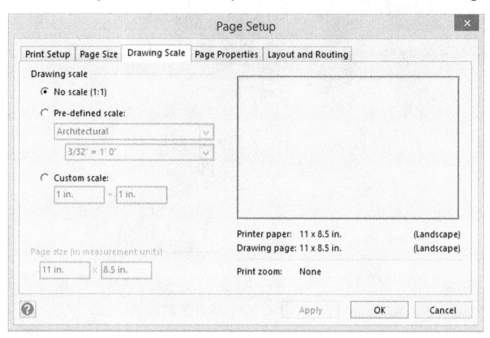

The Page Properties tab allows you to choose the name, type, background, and measurement units of the drawing.

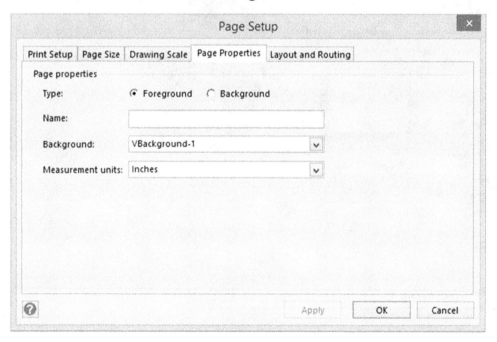

The Page Properties tab allows you to indicate routine and line jumps for your diagram.

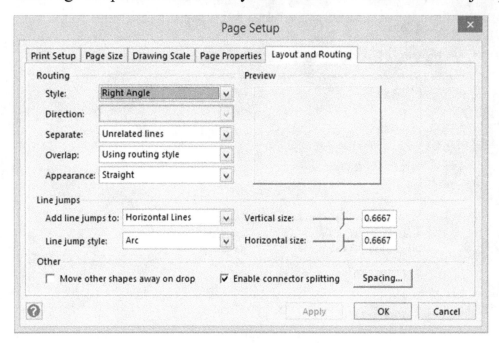

The Shadows tab allows you to add an overall shadow to the diagram.

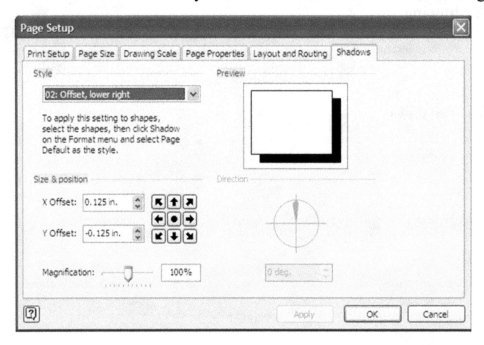

Saving Your Drawing as a Picture

You can save your drawing as any of the following formats to share with other viewers who may not have Visio installed on their computers:

- Web Drawing (for use on Visio Services with SharePoint)
- PNG
- EMF Metafile
- JPEG
- Scalable Vector Graphics
- XML Drawing
- HTML Page
- AutoCAD
- PDF
- XPS

Use the following procedure to save the drawing as a picture.

Step 1: Select the **FILE** tab on the Ribbon.

Step 2: Select the **Share** item.

Step 3: Select the **Change File Type** under **File Types**.

Step 4: Select the **Graphic File Type**.

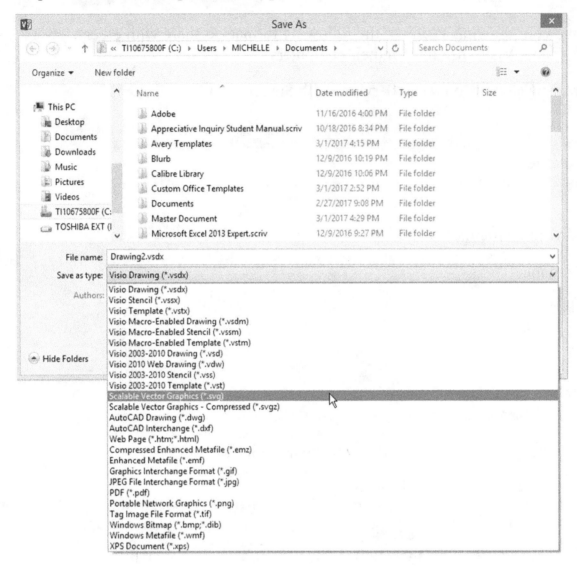

Printing Your Drawing

The Backstage View allows you to open a print preview, quick print using the default settings, or open the Print dialog box to set your print options.

Use the following procedure to open the Print dialog box.

Step 1: Select the **FILE** tab on the Ribbon.

Step 2: Select the **Print** item.

Step 3: Select **Print**.

E-mailing Your Drawing

Visio 2013 makes it easier than ever to share your files. You can attach the drawing to an E-mail in either the Visio format, PDF format, or XPS format. You can also email a link of the drawing if the drawing is saved to a shared folder.

Use the following procedure to email a drawing.

Step 1: Select the FILE tab on the Ribbon.

Step 2: Select the **Share** item.

Step 3: Select **Send Using E-mail**.

Step 4: Select **Send as Attachment.**

Additional Titles

The Technical Skill Builder series of books covers a variety of technical application skills. For the availability of titles please see https://www.silvercitypublications.com/shop/. Note the Master Class volume contains the Essentials, Advanced, and Expert (when available) editions.

Current Titles

Microsoft Excel 2013 Essentials

Microsoft Excel 2013 Advanced

Microsoft Excel 2013 Expert

Microsoft Excel 2013 Master Class

Microsoft Word 2013 Essentials

Microsoft Word 2013 Advanced

Microsoft Word 2013 Expert

Microsoft Word 2013 Master Class

Microsoft Project 2010 Essentials

Microsoft Project 2010 Advanced

Microsoft Project 2010 Expert

Microsoft Project 2010 Master Class

Microsoft Visio 2010 Essentials

Microsoft Visio 2010 Advanced

Microsoft Visio 2010 Master Class

Coming Soon

Microsoft Access 2013 Essentials

Microsoft Access 2013 Advanced

Microsoft Access 2013 Expert

Microsoft Access 2013 Master Class

Microsoft PowerPoint 2013 Essentials

Microsoft PowerPoint 2013 Advanced

Microsoft PowerPoint 2013 Expert

Microsoft PowerPoint 2013 Master Class

Microsoft Outlook 2013 Essentials

Microsoft Outlook 2013 Advanced

Microsoft Outlook 2013 Expert

Microsoft Outlook 2013 Master Class

Microsoft Publisher 2013 Essentials

Microsoft Publisher 2013 Advanced

Microsoft Publisher 2013 Master Class

Windows 7 Essentials

Windows 8 Essentials

www.ingramcontent.com/pod-product-compliance
Lightning Source LLC
Chambersburg PA
CBHW060204060326

40690CB00018B/4249